FOOTBALL JOKES

RULE

> **Hi,** pleased to meet you.

> We hope you enjoy our football joke book.

THIS IS A WELBECK CHILDREN'S BOOK
Published in 2021 by Welbeck Children's Books Limited
An imprint of the Welbeck Publishing Group
20 Mortimer Street, London W1T 3JW
Text © Welbeck Publishing Limited 2021
Design & Illustration © 2021 Dan Green
ISBN: 978-1-78312-630-9

Writer: Simon Mugford
Designer and Illustrator: Dan Green
Design manager: Sam James
Executive editor: Suhel Ahmed
Production: Arlene Alexander

A catalogue record for this book is available from the British Library.

Printed in the UK
10 9 8 7 6 5 4 3 2 1

Statistics and records correct as of July 2021

FOOTBALL SUPERSTARS

FOOTBALL JOKES RULE

SIMON MUGFORD   DAN GREEN

CONTENTS

What do you get if you cross a **PREMIER LEAGUE**-winning defender with a deliveryman?

VIRGIL *VAN DRIVER*.

WELL, I DELIVER TROPHIES TO ANFIELD!

LIVERPOOL

Who is a **GOAL MACHINE** in Germany's Bundesliga?

ROBOT LEWANDOWSKI.

Must. Score. Goals!

Why did Aaron Wan-Bissaka miss a big game for Manchester United?

BECAUSE HE WAS STILL *RIGHT-BACK* IN THE DRESSING ROOM.

Which **PREMIER LEAGUE CLUB** gets the most rain at their stadium?

***WET* HAM.**

LIONEL MESSI never enjoyed playing in cup competitions in Spain.

HE COULDN'T *COPA* WITH THE PRESSURE.

GOTCHA!

Which **TV QUIZ SHOW** should the team second in the league, trying to overtake the leaders, watch?

THE CHASE.

KARIM BENZEMA, **GARETH BALE** and **CRISTIANO RONALDO** won loads of Champions League titles at **REAL MADRID**. They were nicknamed the **BBC.**

Karim Benzema

Gareth Bale

Cristiano Ronaldo

THE COACH GAVE THEM A *'LICENCE FEE'* TO ATTACK.

I PAY MY TV LICENCE FEE EVERY YEAR, OR EVERY 12 MONTHS, **I FORGET** WHICH IT IS...

How has **CRISTIANO RONALDO** netted

so many times for his country?

BECAUSE HE'S
A LEGENDARY
PORTU-GOAL
SCORER.

What happened to the **PREMIER LEAGUE PLAYER** who was late for **KICK-OFF** because he was reading a Harry Potter novel?

THE REFEREE BOOKED HIM AND HE HAD A *SPELL* ON THE TOUCHLINE.

WHY DID THE CHAMPIONSHIP TEAM HAVE A **HUGE LADDER?**

SO THEY COULD *CLIMB* UP TO THE PREMIER LEAGUE.

WAYNE ROONEY reckons he is the Premier League's **G.O.A.T.**

HE MUST BE *KID*-DING!

WHO IS THE **BIGGEST** PLAYER AT CHELSEA?

MASON *MOUNT*-AIN.

In the **SCOTTISH PREMIERSHIP**, why do players like **SHOOTING** from outside the box at Ibrox?

SO THEY CAN SCORE A *LONG* RANGER.

What's the **SCARIEST** part of **FOOTBALL**?

WHEN A GAME GOES TO *SUDDEN DEATH* PENALTIES.

AFTER BEING **KNOCKED OUT** OF THE CUP, THE MANAGER TOLD HIS PLAYERS TO LOOK AT THEIR **DIVISION TABLE** CLOSELY.

STRANGE. **WHY?**

BECAUSE THEY NOW HAD TO *CONCENTRATE* ON THE LEAGUE

16

CHAPTER 2

GAME GIGGLES

17

Which player is always **COMPLAINING** during a game?

MOAN SALAH.

A **GOALKEEPER** made brilliant saves in the first half of the game, but was **TOTAL RUBBISH** in the second half.

HE WAS A *SEMI-*PROFESSIONAL PLAYER.

Why do **FOOTBALL PLAYERS** always **SUCCEED** in school?

THEY KNOW HOW TO USE THEIR *HEADS*.

Why are **CHRISTMAS** fixtures always the coldest?

IT'S BECAUSE THE GAMES ARE PLAYED IN *DECEMBRRRRR!*

The **MANCHESTER UNITED TEAM** could not stop **LAUGHING** while eating their pre-game meal.

THE FOOD *TASTED FUNNY*.

At the end of a game, what does the **GOALKEEPER** always say to the ball?

CATCH YOU LATER.

WHY DID THE FOOTBALLER START **MUNCHING** THE PITCH BEFORE A GAME?

HE WAS TOLD TO EAT HIS *GREENS* TO STAY HEALTHY.

22

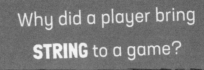

Why did a player bring **STRING** to a game?

SO HE COULD *TIE* THE SCORE.

WHY CAN'T **PIGS PLAY** A GAME OF FOOTBALL?

BECAUSE THEY ALWAYS *HOG* THE BALL.

TWO TEAMS play a game. One team wins, but **NO MAN** on either team scores a goal or a penalty in shootout. How is this possible?

BECAUSE THEY ARE BOTH *WOMEN'S* TEAMS.

Why were the **STAR WARS FANS** lost on the way to watch a game?

THEY TOOK AN _R2-DETOUR_ TO THE GROUND.

The **TEDDY MASCOT** left the football game because his side was losing.

HE COULDN'T _BEAR_ THE DEFEAT.

What car does **MANCHESTER UNITED'S** No.10 striker drive to a game?

Players often **SHAKE HANDS** with the other **TEAM** before a match kicks off.

IT HELPS THEM GET TO *GRIPS* WITH THE OPPOSITION.

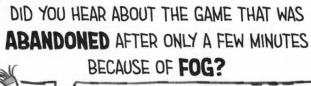

DID YOU HEAR ABOUT THE GAME THAT WAS **ABANDONED** AFTER ONLY A FEW MINUTES BECAUSE OF **FOG?**

I LOVE FOOTBALL JOKES

THE FANS **MIST** ALL THE ACTION.

I'M GOING TO WATCH A GAME IN **SOUTH YORKSHIRE** IN MIDWEEK.

SHEFFIELD WEDNESDAY?

NO, **BARNSLEY ON TUESDAY.**

A team gave all their midfielders **HOSEPIPES** to use during a game.

THEY WANTED TO *FLOOD* **THE CENTRE OF THE PITCH.**

CHAPTER 3

TEAM TICKLES

Which **TEAM** do sheep support?

BAAAAAAAAH-RCELONA

UN-**BAAAAH**-LIEVABLE!

How many **PUSH-UPS** can a **FOOTBALLER** do?

ALL OF THEM.

DOES THIS COUNT?

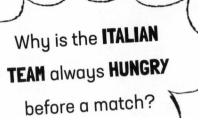

Why is the **ITALIAN TEAM** always **HUNGRY** before a match?

THEY ARE DESPERATE FOR *A PIZZA THE ACTION*.

DID YOU HEAR THAT **FATHER CHRISTMAS PLAYS FOOTY**? HIS TEAM NEVER PASS OR ASSIST EACH OTHER, THOUGH.

THEY HAVE A VERY *S-ELF-ISH* WAY OF PLAYING!

Why did the **FOOTBALL TEAM** give up their **BALLET LESSONS?**

IT WAS _TUTU_ DIFFICULT FOR THEM.

THIS IS MORE LIKE **BREAK DANCING!**

How did the **BRAZIL TEAM** win **STRICTLY COME DANCING?**

BECAUSE THEY ARE THE _SAMBA BOYS_.

Why was the **TEAM** two weeks late for kick-off?

THEY WERE TOO BUSY PLAYING _FORTNITE_.

The West Ham team lives at the **TOP** of a **TOWER BLOCK**. What TV show do the residents below them watch?

HOMES UNDER THE HAMMERS.

BARBER

The ambitious **FOOTBALL CLUB** made all its players have **SHAVED HAIRSTYLES**.

THEY SAID IT WAS A _SHORT CUT_ TO SUCCESS.

Who **PROTECTS** all the international teams at **FIFA'S MAJOR TOURNAMENT** every four years?

THE WORLD COPS.

Which **SOUTH AMERICAN TEAM** has the youngest players?

BOCA JUNIORS.

WHICH LONDON **FOOTBALL TEAM** IS ALWAYS DOING THE WASHING UP?
CRYSTAL PLATES.

CHAPTER 4

MEDICAL MADNESS

What do you call **TWO AMBULANCE**

drivers at a football ground?

PAIR-OF-MEDICS.

Players complained of **UPSET BELLIES** after eating lots of brownies.

THE MEDICAL STAFF TOLD THEM THEY WERE SUFFERING FROM *STOMACH-CAKE*.

A TEAM DECIDED TO CHANGE THEIR KIT DESIGN TO ONE WITH COLOURED SPOTS, BUT IT MADE THEIR BODIES ITCH.

THE TEAM DOCTOR RECKONED IT WAS A *RASH* **DECISION.**

45

Where do **FOOTBALLERS** buy their medicine?

BOOTS.

A **GOALKEEPER** WAS IN AGONY AFTER PUTTING **CONCRETE** IN HIS EARS.

THE DOCTOR SAID HE WAS *HARD OF HEARING.*

Harry Kane suffered **NASTY TACKLES** below his knees in both home and away **CHAMPIONS LEAGUE** semi-final games.

HE WAS INJURED IN *BOTH LEGS.*

When **MESSI** was a boy, he had to take medication to help him **GROW** over a number of years.

DOCTORS TOLD HIM TO BE A *LITTLE PATIENT.*

The footballer went to the **DOCTOR** with **TERRIBLE PAIN** in his **TUMMY**.
He said: "Aaaa, eeeh, I, Oh! You..."

THE DOCTOR REPLIED: "I THINK YOU HAVE *IRRITABLE VOWEL SYNDROME.*"

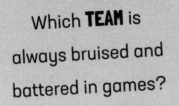

Which **TEAM** is always bruised and battered in games?

Q.P.ARRGGHH!

DOCTOR, YOU'VE GOT TO HELP ME GET OUT OF THIS **TREATMENT ROOM** AND FINALLY BACK ON THE PITCH!

SURE, THE *EXIT DOOR* IS OVER THERE!

Why were **PLAYERS** from the team at the bottom of the **PREMIER LEAGUE** always getting headaches?

FROM COUNTING ALL THE GOALS THEY LET IN.

Doctors don't like it when **PLAYERS SLIDE** in a **GOAL CELEBRATION** and risk injury.

THEY SAY THERE IS NO _KNEED_ FOR IT.

A player went to the **DOCTOR** because he was worried about **FALLING ASLEEP** during games.

"WELL, YOU SNOOZE YOU LOSE!" THE DOC WARNED HIM.

Which part of a **STADIUM** never stays the same?

THE CHANGING ROOM.

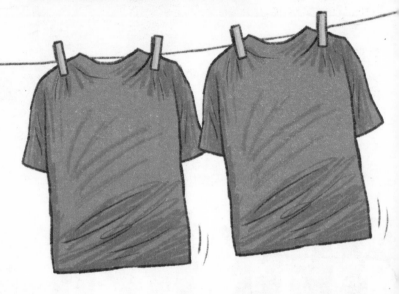

Which part of a stadium
SMELLS the nicest?

THE 'SCENTER' SPOT.

When **MANCHESTER CITY** lose at home, the City fans always leave early.

THEY'VE JUST *ETI-HAD* ENOUGH.

HEY, DON'T GO!

IS IT INJURY TIME OR HOME TIME?

WHAT IS THE MOST **ANCIENT** FOOTY PLACE?

OLD TRAFFORD.

Why did Italy hero **FRANCESCO TOTTI** never like playing away from his club ground?

FOR HIM THERE WAS NO PLACE LIKE ROME.

Why have **BARCELONA** got the most modern **STADIUM?**

BECAUSE IT'S *THE NEW CAMP.*

Why did all the **TOTTENHAM FANS** have a **DISCO** at their stadium?

THEY ALWAYS ENJOY A BIG *ATTEN-DANCE.*

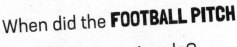

When did the **FOOTBALL PITCH** become a triangle?

AFTER SOMEONE TOOK A CORNER.

TRIANGLE? DOES THAT MEAN THERE ARE THREE SIDES PLAYING?

Did you hear about the **INTERNATIONAL STADIUM** that was **UNDERWATER?**

THERE WAS A PROBLEM WITH THE _FLOOD-LIGHTS._

Where would **HENRY VIII**, **RICHARD III** and **CHARLES II** like to watch football?

AT LEICESTER'S _KING POWER_ STADIUM.

SOUTH KOREA'S NATIONAL STADIUM IS A GREAT PLACE TO CELEBRATE GOALS.

WHY'S THAT?

IT'S THE LIFE AND _SEOUL_ OF THE PARTY!

Where do **LIONS** go to watch a game?

THE DEN.

EVERTON'S **STARS** KEPT RUNNING INTO SLIDES, SEE-SAWS, SWINGS, CLIMBING FRAMES, BENCHES AND **DOG WALKERS**.

THAT'S THE TROUBLE WITH PLAYING AT GOODISON **PARK**.

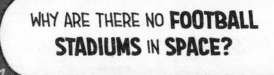

The **FRANCE TEAM** got lost on the way to their **STADIUM.**

ARC DE TRIOMPHE

PARIS

EIFFEL TOWER

IT WAS OKAY THOUGH, BECAUSE KYLIAN **M-MAP-PE** SHOWED THEM THE WAY.

CHAPTER 6

SPORTY STORIES

69

In June and July, an **ENGLISH TEAM** got on their bikes and took a **FERRY** across the Channel.

THEY THOUGHT THEY WERE TOLD TO GO ON THE TOUR DE FRANCE... BUT ACTUALLY THEY WERE GOING ON A PRE-SEASON *TOUR TO FRANCE!*

Why did the **GYMNASTIC COACH** teach players to spin and **TUMBLE** on the pitch?

SO THEY COULD BE *ROLL MODELS.*

Why won't footballers tell **JOKES** while **ICE-SKATING?**

BECAUSE THE ICE MIGHT *CRACK UP.*

Why were the players **JUMPING** around the **SPORTS TRACK** while doing seven different events?

THEY WERE COMPETING IN THE *HOP-TATHLON.*

WHAT TIME DID THE **FOOTBALLERS** GO TO **WIMBLEDON** TO WATCH THE MEN'S FINAL?

AT *TEN-NIS* O'CLOCK.

MY FIRST TENNIS BOOK

AND AT **WHAT TIME** DID THEY LEAVE THE COURT?

WHEN THE GAME WAS *WIMBLE-DONE.*

Why were the players trying to **SIT ON TOP** of each other?

THEY WANTED TO PLAY *SQUASH.*

A team did some athletics **TRAINING** in pre-season. One player decided to wear a big **PULLOVER** for it.

HE THOUGHT IT WOULD MAKE HIM A *LONG JUMPER.*

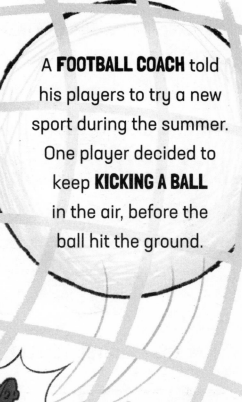

A **FOOTBALL COACH** told his players to try a new sport during the summer. One player decided to keep **KICKING A BALL** in the air, before the ball hit the ground.

THE COACH TOLD HIM HE WASN'T PLAYING A NEW SPORT. THE FOOTBALLER SAID IT WAS... *VOLLEY BALL.*

A striker went to the **GYM** to improve his strength and power. He kept **PICKING UP** the barbell, **PUTTING IT DOWN** for a long time and then picking it up again much later.

HE WAS WAIT LIFTING.

Where does Virgil van Dijk go swimming?

AT THE *LIVER-POOL.*

WHY DIDN'T THE **FOOTBALL** FANS ENJOY THE **WRESTLING** MATCH?

BECAUSE THEY THOUGHT IT WAS JUST TWO SPORTS PEOPLE WITHOUT ***TROUSERS*** FIGHTING FOR A ***BELT!***

What do **GOLFERS** and former England striker **JERMAIN DEFOE** have in common?

THEY HAVE BOTH GOT THROUGH LOTS OF *CLUBS*.

What do you get if you cross a Formula One team with a **FOOTBALL CLUB?**

TOTTENHAM HOT WHEELS.

Why do **FOOTBALLERS** boot their **BIKES** a lot?

TO IMPROVE THEIR
BICYCLE KICKS.

KEEP THE NOISE DOWN, LADS!

The football team went **BOWLING** but they didn't **SPEAK** to each other.

IT WAS SO QUIET THEY COULD HEAR A *TEN-PIN* DROP.

Why are the Norwich players good on the trampoline?

BECAUSE THEY ARE ALWAYS *GOING UP, THEN DOWN, UP, THEN DOWN.*

WHAT IS **ROBERT LEWANDOWSKI'S** FAVOURITE SPORT?

THE *POLE* VAULT.

Which other sport are **FOOTBALLERS TERRIBLE** at?

BAD-MINTON.

What do you get if you cross an **ARGENTINA LEGEND** with a **26-MILE** running race?

A DIEGO MARADONA-THON.

CHAPTER 7

MANAGER MAYHEM

Why did the **MANAGER** give his team **SUPERGLUE**?

HE WANTED THEM TO ALL STICK TOGETHER ON THE PITCH.

What happened when **MO SALAH** had his Golden Boot **STOLEN**?

HE CALLED THE KLOPPS TO REPORT THE CRIME.

Why did **JURGEN KLOPP** remove his hat after a **BIG WIN?**

TO **CAP OFF** A GOOD VICTORY.

Did you hear about the **UNHAPPY** team that **FLEW** to all their away games instead of travelling by bus?

THEY REALLY DIDN'T LIKE THEIR *COACH.*

STADIUM 300KM

87

Why did the **MANAGER** give his players boxing gloves?

THEY WERE IN A *KNOCKOUT* **COMPETITION.**

Why was the **FOOTBALL TEAM** so feeble?

THE MANAGER PLAYED AN *UNDER-STRENGTH* **SIDE.**

Why did the manager **REFUSE** to let a **CAR PLAY** in his team?

BECAUSE IT ONLY HAD *ONE BOOT.*

What do **PEP GUARDIOLA** and Nike have in common?

THEY BOTH MAKE *EXCELLENT TRAINERS.*

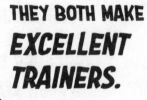

Why did **GARETH SOUTHGATE** take his England players to a **RESTAURANT?**

BECAUSE THEY HAD JUST PLAYED *HUNGARY.*

Why did the American MLS manager say his team was full of star players?

HE WAS IN CHARGE OF *THE GALAXY*.

WHAT DID THE **SPANISH FANS** SAY WHEN THEIR **MANAGER** WAS SACKED?

VALEN-SEE-YA!

Which **LIVERPOOL STAR** will make a great coach in the future?

SADIO ***MANÉ-GER.***

WHY DO MANAGERS BRING **A SPADE** TO EVERY GAME?

BECAUSE THEY'RE IN THE ***DUGOUT.***

After the match, why was the **COACH** talking to the **GOAL FRAME**?

HE WAS GIVING A *POST MATCH* INTERVIEW.

GOAL GAGS

This **MAN. CITY STRIKER** has so much cash and notes in his wallet.

IT'S BECAUSE HE'S PAID IN *STERLING*.

99

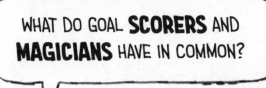

WHAT DO GOAL **SCORERS** AND **MAGICIANS** HAVE IN COMMON?

THEY BOTH DO *HAT-TRICKS.*

BELGIUM played brothers **EDEN**, **THORGAN** and **KYLIAN** in their attack.

THEY HAD A *TRIPLE HAZARD* **UP FRONT.**

Legendary striker **ZLATAN IBRAHIMOVIC** loves telling a story about his little horse.

HE HAS ALWAYS LIKED HIS *PONY TALE.*

Forwards don't score at Halloween.

THEY CAN'T BEAT THE *GHOUL-KEEPER.*

Why was the Man. United striker doing **KARATE KICKS** and **JUDO MOVES?**

HE WAS PRACTISING HIS *ANTHONY MARTIAL-ARTS.*

The **NO.9** refused to do his job and play for his team.

HE SAID HE WAS ON *STRIKE-R.*

Goal scorers are so **NOISY** and **LOUD** in the penalty box.

THREE UP FRONT? OKAY BOSS!

Why does manager **MARCELO BIELSA** play three strikers at the start of a game?

SO THAT HIS TEAM TAKES AN EARLY *LEEDS*.

CHAPTER 9

VIP

(VERY IMPORTANT PLAYERS)

Who is the **FASTEST** Liverpool player of all time?

IAN RUSH.

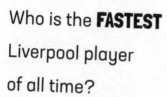

Who is the quickest **MAN. UNITED** player of all time?

HURRY MAGUIRE.

Which **FAMOUS** Liverpool striker always scored in the wrong net?

MICHAEL OWN GOAL.

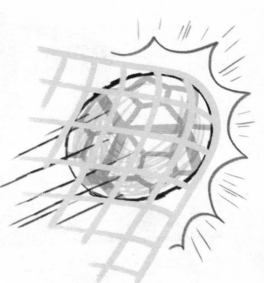

Which former **ENGLAND CAPTAIN** played like a midfield tiger?

STEVEN GERR-RAARRGGHH!

MY SKILLS WERE **PURR-FECT!**

What do you get if you cross France **GOALKEEPING LEGEND** Hugo Lloris with a computer monitor?

A SCREEN SAVER.

Why do millions of **OLD LADIES** follow Neymar on social media?

HE IS VERY POPULAR ON *INSTA-GRAN.*

AFTER **RETIRING,** WHICH MAN. UNITED WINGER BECAME AN AIRLINE PILOT?

FLYIN' GIGGS.

WHICH BARCELONA AND SPAIN MIDFIELD HERO MUNCHES **DIGESTIVES** AND **CUSTARD CREAMS?**

SERGIO BISCUITS.

At the start of this decade, why did all the world's top players go to the opticians?

THEY NEEDED TO HAVE *20-20* VISION.

Why does Virgil van Dijk never give up in an international game?

BECAUSE HE PLAYS FOR THE *NEVER-LANDS.*

Messi had an idea to grow a
beard, but he wasn't totally sure.

**IT SOON STARTED TO *GROW
ON HIM*, THOUGH.**

Why did former international boss **JOACHIM LÖW** have the best job?

BECAUSE HE HAD GER-*MANY* GREAT PLAYERS TO PICK FROM.

WHY DO DE BRUYNE, MAHREZ, FODEN AND SILVA SPARKLE SO MUCH AT MAN. CITY?

THEY MAKE A MIDFIELD *DIAMOND.*

CHAPTER 10

SILLY SOCCER STUFF

The **SCARECROW FOOTBALLER** was given lots of special awards.

HE WON THEM FOR BEING
OUT-STANDING IN HIS FIELD.

ARE YOU JUST GOING TO STAND THERE, OR HELP?

Why did the team leave the **FA CUP** game half way through the first half?

IT WAS ONLY A QUARTER-FINAL.

Which **ENGLAND DEFENDER** constantly falls over on the pitch?

KIERAN TRIP-PIER.

Can you name the **WOMEN'S PLAYER** who always finishes third in competitions?

LUCY BRONZE.

Why are The **TOFFEES** overweight?

BECAUSE THEY WEIGH AN *EVER-TON*

FAT'S NOT FUNNY.

Who is a **HORSE'S** favourite player?

NEIGH-MAR.

WHY DON'T **SKELETONS** PLAY FOOTBALL?

THEIR *HEART* IS JUST NOT IN IT.

Why was the Chelsea player dropped from the team?

HE COULDN'T **KEPA CLEAN SHEET.**

The French team decided to play without a goalkeeper all season.

THEY WERE CLEARLY TRYING *TOU-LOUSE* EVERY GAME.

What does a striker say at Halloween?

"HAT-TRICK OR TREAT?"

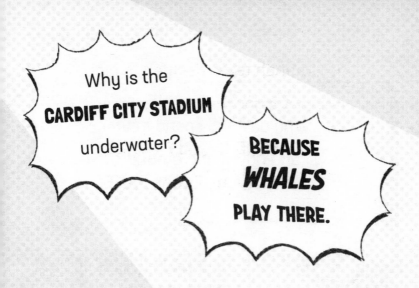

Why is the **CARDIFF CITY STADIUM** underwater?

BECAUSE WHALES PLAY THERE.

What's the most common injury for a defender?

PAIN IN THE CENTRE-BACK.

STRIKERS ARE **A PAIN** FOR DEFENDERS TOO!

ABOUT THE AUTHORS

Simon's first job was at the Science Museum, making paper aeroplanes and blowing bubbles big enough for your dad to stand in. Since then he's written all sorts of books about the stuff he likes, from dinosaurs and rockets, to llamas, loud music and of course, football. Simon has supported Ipswich Town since they won the FA Cup in 1978 (it's true - look it up) and once sat next to Rio Ferdinand on a train. He lives in Kent with his wife and daughter, a dog, cat and two tortoises.

Dan has drawn silly pictures since he could hold a crayon. Then he grew up and started making books about stuff like trucks, space, people's jobs, *Doctor Who* and *Star Wars*. Dan remembers Ipswich Town winning the FA Cup but he didn't watch it because he was too busy making a Viking ship out of brown paper. As a result, he knows more about Vikings than football. Dan lives in Suffolk with his wife, son, daughter and a dog that takes him for very long walks.